Weltkulturerbe
GOSLAR

Goslar Guide

Hans-Günther Grie[...]

VERLAG SCHADACH
LITERATUR AUS DEM HARZ

UNESCO-Weltkulturerbe Goslar – Rammelsberg

Bergleute, Kaiser, Bürger und Künstler prägten das Bild der Goslarer Altstadt, über dem die Kirchtürme wie beschützende Engel aufragen. Der Bergbau war es, der den Kaisern und Königen die Bühne für ihre glanzvollen Auftritte vom 11. bis 13. Jahrhundert bereitete. Der Rammelsberg als "Kupferberg Europas" lieferte das Metall für großartige Bronzeschöpfungen wie Krodoaltar, Kaiserstuhl und Marktbrunnen und als "Bankier" der Herrscher das Geld für die Kaiserpfalz und viele bedeutende Bauten in der Stadt. Vom Goslarer Schicksalsberg lebten auch die Bürger, die mit ihren Fachwerkhäusern den Grundstock für das "Gesamtkunstwerk" Goslar legten.

Der Berg als Quelle und die Altstadt als Folge des Reichtums erhielten 1992 ihren Ritterschlag mit der gemeinsamen Aufnahme in die Liste des UNESCO-Weltkulturerbes. Das 1988 stillgelegte Erzbergwerk Rammelsberg, dessen Anfänge 3 000 Jahre zurückreichen, war das erste deutsche Industriedenkmal, das als Weltkulturerbe anerkannt wurde. Das ehemalige Bergwerk ist selbst ein authentisches Exponat und heute als Bergbaumuseum dank einer hervorragenden Konzeption in der Touristengunst gewissermaßen die "Kaiserpfalz des Bergbaus". Stadt und Berg gehören wie eh und je zusammen und rückten als dezentrales Projekt der Expo 2000 in den Blickpunkt der Weltausstellung mit dem pfiffigen Titel "Expo on the rocks".

An Auszeichnungen ist Goslar reich. So tragen die Kaiserpfalz, das Große Heilige Kreuz (1254), eines des ältesten bürgerlichen Hospitäler in Deutschland, und das mächtige Breite Tor den "Orden" eines Kulturdenkmals "von besonderer nationaler Bedeutung". Der Zusammenklang von außergewöhnlichen Bauwerken, zu

UNESCO World Heritage Goslar – Rammelsberg

Miners, emperors, citizens and artists left their imprint on Goslar's Old Town, over which the church steeples soar like guardian angles. The mines are what provided the emperors and kings with the appropriate stage for their resplendent appearances from the 11th through the 14th centuries. The Rammelsberg as "Europe's Copper Mountain" delivered the metal for tremendous bronze creations such as the Krodo Altar, the Imperial Throne and the Market Fountain and as the "treasurer" of the rulers provided the funds for the Imperial Palace and many important structures in the city. Goslar's "Mountain of Fate" provided the means of living for the citizens who, with their half-timbered houses, were the basis for the "art entirety" Goslar.

The mountain as source and the Old Town as outcome of the wealth were knighted in 1992 when they were jointly entered on the UNESCO World Cultural Heritage List. The ore mines of the Rammelsberg, closed down in 1988, whose beginning goes back 3000 years, was the first German industrial monument to be recognised as a world cultural heritage monument. The former mine is itself an authentic exponent and today, as a mining museum, thanks to an outstanding conception, has tourist popularity as a kind of "Imperial Palace of Mining". Town and mountain belong together as they always have, and moved into the limelight as a decentralised project of the Expo 2000 world's fair with the catchy theme "Expo on the rocks".

Goslar is rich in awards. The Imperial Palace, the Great Holy Cross hospital (1254), one of the oldest citizen's almshouses in Germany, and the huge Broad Gate are all cultural monuments" of particular national importance". The harmony of exceptional

denen auch die Kirchen gehören, und bescheidenen Fachwerkhäusern macht im Gegensatz zu mancher anderen Stadt den Reiz Goslars aus. Goslar ist kein Museum, in dem nur die Vergangenheit konserviert wird, sondern hier hat auch die Gegenwart ihren Platz. Mit dem Goslarer Kaiserring, einem international renommierten Kunstpreis, schreibt man die Kunst fort. Werke weltweit bedeutender Künstler wie Henry Moore, Max Bill, Richard Serra oder Victor Vasarely stehen inmitten der mittelalterlichen Stadt. Christo verpackte den letzten Förderwagen ("Hunt") des Bergwerks, der heute im Bergbaumuseum steht. Im Mönchehaus-Museum für moderne Kunst, einem Fachwerkbau von 1528, kommt es zur Begegnung mit arrivierten und jungen Künstlern der Moderne.

Dieser Goslar-Führer ist ein sachkundiger Cicerone in die Geschichte und zu den Juwelen der Kaiserstadt. Mit dem Heimatforscher Hans-Günther Griep, Hausforscher und Volkskundler, wurde ein ausgewiesener Fachmann für die unterschiedlichen Aspekte der Stadtlandschaft als Autor gewonnen. Die Fotos von Volker Schadach und Regine Schulz vermitteln dank ihrer Brillanz ein eindrucksvolles Bild des tausendjährigen Goslars.

Mit Pfalzbezirk und Marktplatz begegnen sich zudem die kaiserlichen und bürgerlichen "Machtzentren". Am Markt sind das Rathaus mit dem Huldigungssaal und das Gildehaus der Fernhandelskaufleute, die "Kaiserworth", bis heute unwiderstehliche Touristenmagnete.

structures, to which the churches also belong, and humble half timber houses makes Goslar, in contrast to some other towns, especially attractive.

Goslar is no museum, in which only the past is conserved, but rather where the here and now also has its place. With the Goslar Kaiser Ring, an internationally renowned art prize, art is projected forward. Works by artists of world renown such as Henry Moore, Max Bill, Richard Serra or Victor Vasarely stand in the middle of the medieval town. Christo wrapped the last cart of ore ("Hunt") from the mines, which today is in the mining museum. In the Mönchehaus Museum for Modern Art, a half timber house from 1528, established and young artists of the contemporary rub shoulders.

This Goslar guide is a factual "Cicerone" of the history and treasures of the Imperial town. With the homeland researcher Hans-Günther Griep, ethnic and community researcher, a proven specialist in the different aspects of the cityscape has been won. The photos from Volker Schadach and Regine Schulz give an impressive picture, thanks to their brilliance, of the 1000-year-old Goslar.

With the Imperial Palatinate and the Market Square a meeting of the imperial and communal "power centres" takes place. On the Market the town hall with the Hall of Homage and the guild house of the wholesale merchants, the Kaiserworth, are today irresistible tourist magnets.

Dr. Ursula Müller

Geschichte

Es ist schon ein schwieriges Unterfangen, einem Besucher in kurzer Zeit alles Wissenswerte über Goslar nahezubringen. Zu viele Facetten besitzt diese Stadt. Die wissenschaftliche Literatur füllt schon viele Bücherschränke, und der Born ist lange noch nicht ausgeschöpft. Noch schwieriger wird der Versuch, sich auf bemerkenswerte Abschnitte zu beschränken, denn auf fast allen Gebieten ist besonders Wichtiges zu finden. Jede Wissenschaft findet hier Forschungsangebote und -aufgaben, jedes Steckenpferd sein Futter.

Schon die Landschaft ist von der Natur reich gesegnet. Das fast vollständig aufgeschlagene Buch der Erdgeschichte enthält Bodenschätze aller Art, die weiten Wälder geben einer vielfältigen Fauna und Flora Lebensraum. Seltene Arten haben sich hier erhalten, und manche Tier- und Pflanzengesellschaften, die verloren schienen, konnten wieder eingebürgert werden.

Der Harz als natürliche Barriere bildet auch eine Grenze zwischen Völkerschaften, die Volkstum, Glauben und Brauch geprägt haben: Niedersachsen und Thüringer, Ostfalen und Anhaltiner-Sachsen. Als Baumwald und Reichsforst war der Harz jedoch nicht nur eine Grenze, sondern zugleich auch ein Bindeglied deutscher Geschichte.

Der Harzraum mit seinen ausgedehnten Waldungen und der fruchtbaren Börde am Nordrand sowie der goldenen Aue am Südrand war zu allen Zeiten ein Kernland Europas.

Hier kreuzten sich die Naturstraßen und Völkerstraßen auf dem Weg von Skandinavien nach Italien und vom Frankenland zum Slawenland. Zwar war der Bergrücken kein Siedlungs-

History

Any attempt to tell a visitor everything worth knowing about Goslar in a short time is bound to fail. There are just too many sides and sights to this city. The scholarly literature on Goslar is already filling endless bookshelves and still there is no end in sight. And any effort to limit oneself to the more remarkable sections of the city's past seems even more futile as almost every imaginable field of interest claims some unneglectable aspect of vital importance. In Goslar, any science finds its research topic, any hobby horse its fodder.

For those who can read the signs, the surrounding countryside is an open book in itself. A long geological past offers natural resources of just about any kind, the extensive woods are home to a greatly varying fauna and flora. Many a rare species have survived here, and some animals and plants that seemed on the virge of extinction could be re-established in their former habitats.

The Harz mountain has also been a natural barrier between the peoples who shaped the ways of life, the beliefs, and the customs of this land: the Lower Saxons and Thuringians, the East Falians and the Anhalt Saxons. Yet the vast forests under the direct rule of the Reich were not only border line but also a unifying link in the course of German history.

The Harz region with its seemingly endless woods, the fertile soils at its northern rim and the mellow grasslands to its south has always been at the heart of Europe.

Here the natural roads from Scandinavia in the north to Italy in the south, from the Frankish countries in the west to Slavic countries in the east intersected. Although the mountains

land, aber die notwendige Ergänzung des Bauernlandes im Umkreis, und viele Verbindungen führten hinüber. Nur an den Talausgängen lagen kleine Ortschaften.

In die Reihe solcher, für uns zunächst namenlosen Siedlungsplätze gehörte auch das heutige Goslar. Hier haben seit der mittleren Steinzeit Menschen gewohnt und gearbeitet. Als Jäger und Sammler durchzogen sie das Bergland, mindestens seit der Bronzezeit waren sie als Bauern auf den Lößböden sesshaft und betrieben Bergbau. Wenn man von unsicheren Nachrichten der antiken Schriftsteller absieht, tritt unser Raum im Rahmen der Eroberungen und Missionsfeldzüge der Franken in das Licht der Geschichte, zunächst im Zusammenhang mit den Kämpfen zwischen Sachsen und Thüringern um 530, dann durch Vorstöße der Franken selbst 747 durch Pippin, 775 und 780 durch Karl den Großen. Die damals eingeführte staatliche Ordnung bildet bis in unsere Tage hinein eine Grundlage weltlicher Machtreviere.

Bis 968 war Goslar eine kleine Siedlung, wie es damals viele gegeben haben wird. Es gelang jedoch, aus dem über Tage ausgehenden, also weithin sichtbaren, leuchtend bunten Erzlager des Rammelsberges auch das begehrte Metall, vor allem Silber, ertragreich herauszuschmelzen.

Die Erschließung des Rammelsberger Erzlagers muß auf die Menschen jener Zeit wie ein Goldrausch gewirkt haben. Viele suchten hier ein neues Glück, vielleicht auch einen Ausweg aus den Zwängen einer Leibeigenschaft. Der Abbau des gewaltigen Erzklumpens war schwer, brachte aber in dem ersten Jahrhundert keine technischen Schwierigkeiten. Der Gewinn dürfte entsprechend hoch gewesen sein. In wenigen Jahrzehnten entstand so die größte Stadt außerhalb des

were not settled themselves, they still served as a natural resource to the surrounding farmland. Roads crossed the mountains, and small hamlets grew in the lower valleys at their feet.

Goslar, too, once started out as such a nameless collection of dwellings. From the middle Stone Age on men have lived and worked here. As hunters and gatherer they constantly roamed the primeval forests, and with the advent of the Bronze Age they settled down, began to farm the fertile soils and started mining. Yet not more than distant rumours enter the writings of ancient historians. It is only with the conquests and missionary campaigns of the Franks that the area begins to enter the limelight of written history. A first footnote appears around 530 with reports on the fights between Saxons and Thuringians. Frankish expeditions take place under Pippin in 747, and again in 775 and 780 by Charlemagne himself. The borders drawn then have continued to define spheres of influence up to our days.

Until 968 Goslar was just another small hamlet among many. But when ways and means where found to exploit the colourful ore veins at the Rammelsberg's surface and when the smelters began to produce the much sought after metals, in particular silver, its fate began to change.

Opening up the ore deposits of the Rammelsberg must have been kind of a gold-rush for the people of those days. Many tried to make their fortune, and some also may have looked for a way to escape the forces of servitude. While it was hard work to extract the large chunks of ore from the ground, it did not provide any technological difficulties during the first century and profits were correspondingly high. So within a few decades the small hamlet grew into the largest city outside the

Blick von Norden nach Süden über Riechenberg und Goslar zum Harz mit dem Brocken als höchstem Gipfel.

A View from the north to the south over Riechenberg and Goslar towards the Harz and the Brocken peak.

untergegangenen Römerreiches. Schon 1009 konnte in einer neuen Pfalz an der Stelle des erhaltenen alten Kaiserhauses eine erste Reichsversammlung stattfinden.

Die Stadt bekam ihren Namen von dem Flüßchen Gose, das hier den Harz verläßt. Er läßt sich sprachlich von dem Begriff für schnell fließendes Wasser ableiten, der z.B. noch in "gießen" oder "Gosse" erhalten ist. Hinzu kam der fränkische Wortstamm "lar" für eine Niederlassung.

Um 1050 versuchte Kaiser Heinrich III. sogar, hier eine ständige Residenz einzurichten. Selbst der Papst kam nach Goslar, um den Kaiser zu besuchen, und die Chronisten berichten von Goslar als dem nordischen Rom.

former Roman empire. Already by 1009 a new imperial palace had been built to replace the old mansion and the first imperial diet at Goslar could be held.

The name of the city is derived from "Gose", the name of the creek running through it. "Gose" is said to come from the term for 'fast running water', a meaning still found in gießen (pour) and Gosse (gutter), while "lar" is the root of the frankish word for settlement.

Around 1050 emperor Heinrich III. even intended to set up a permanent residence. Even the pope once travelled here to see the his world counterpart, while the chronicles tell of Goslar as the Rome of the North.

Im Herzen Europas gelegen, waren Goslar und der Harz über mehr als drei Jahrhunderte das Zentrum des Heiligen Römischen Reiches Deutscher Nation. Die Kaiserpfalz Goslar wurde, gestärkt durch den Silbersegen aus den Gruben des Rammelsberges, zur heimlichen Hauptstadt, zum nordischen Rom.

In der mittelalterlichen Großstadt Goslar erstarkte aber auch das Bürgertum und schuf sich Gesetze und Ordnungen, die weithin in Mitteldeutschland und im Osten Vorbild wurden und Geltung besaßen. Die Stadtfreiheit der Bürger bestand hier schon so lange, daß sie nicht mehr besonders herausgestellt werden mußte, als sich andere Städte in Deutschland entsprechende Privilegien verleihen ließen.

Im 11. Jahrhundert entwickelten sich dann schnell der Marktbezirk mit der Pfarrkirche St. Cosmas und Damian, das Handwerkerviertel mit der Kirche St. Jakobi und schließlich die Unterstadt mit der St. Stephanikirche. Nachdem 1108 die Pfarrgrenzen innerhalb der bebauten Gebiete festgelegt waren, dürfte die Stadt im topographischen Sinne den Umfang erreicht haben, den die Altstadt bis heute besitzt.

Auch wenn die Befestigungsanlagen erst 1181 mit dem "Burgum am Ruzindore" erstmals erwähnt werden, dürfte um 1100 auch schon der Mauerring bestanden haben, der, von wenigen Ausnahmen abgesehen, über die Jahrhunderte seinen Verlauf beibehalten hat.

Aus den ehemaligen Befestigungsanlagen ist heute der grüne Gürtel der Stadt geworden. Bergwiesen und Wälder bilden den Übergang zu den Harzbergen und gliedern die Neubaugebiete.

Lying literally in the heart of Europe, Goslar and the Harz mountains remained the centre of the Holy Roman Empire of German Nation for more than threehundred years. The imperial palace of Goslar, supported by the silver of the Rammelsberg mines, slowly evolved as the secret capital, the Rome of the North.

But the Middle Age city of Goslar also saw its citizens become a new force in the Reich. The laws and orders they gave themselves soon served as a model for similar developments in central Germany and further east. The freedoms of the city had been in existence for so long that they did not need any special mention anymore when other German towns were still struggling to have such privileges bestowed on them.

During the 11th century the town began to acquire the topographical borders and layout it has retained up to our days, and by 1108 the lines between the different parishes had been firmly set: there was the thriving market district with the market church of St. Cosmas and Damian, the extensive craftsmen's quarters with the church of St. Jacobus, and eastwards the lower town with the church of St. Stephanus.

Although the city's defences with its "Burgum am Rudzindore" (tower at the gate) are not mentioned in the chronicles until 1181, it appears well justified to assume that the ringwall, which changed very little in the course of the century, was already in existence by 1100.

Today these former defences have become the green belt of the city. The surrounding meadows and woods lend some topographical structure to the newer sections of the town and also blend into the mountains beyond.

Marktplatz mit Rathaus und Marktkir-che, dahinter die Kaiserpfalz

The market square with town hall and Market Church, back left the palace

Der Bergbau und der aus den Hütten erzielte große Gewinn sicherten die Entwicklung Goslars zu einer volkreichen Stadt mit sechs Pfarrbezirken. Auch die Kaiser und Könige weilten immer häufiger in der Goslarer Pfalz. Diese wurde prächtig ausgebaut und die Stadtlandschaft im Sinne der Civitas Dei des Kirchenvaters Augustin planmäßig gestaltet. Ein "Kirchenkreuz" gliederte die Stadt, und auf den Randbergen umzog sie ein Kranz von Klöstern und Kapellen. Kaiser Heinrich III. und sein in Goslar geborener Sohn Heinrich IV. waren schließlich so häufig in Goslar, daß man fast von einer ständigen Residenz sprechen konnte. Sie hielten hier bedeutsame Reichstage ab, und 1056 besuchte sogar der Papst Viktor II. den Kaiser in Goslar.

Auf den Reichstagen der Salier- und Hohenstaufen-Kaiser wurde in der Goslarer Kaiserpfalz europäische Geschichte geschrieben.

Zwar wurde Goslar danach nicht von den Kaisern vergessen, und 1252/53 kehrte Wilhelm von Holland noch einmal in der Pfalz ein, aber der Mittelpunkt der Reichsgeschichte war die Stadt nicht mehr. Hier herrschten als Erben der Kaiser nun einige Patriziergeschlechter und die großen Reichsklöster.

Der Reichtum aus Berg und Wald floß nunmehr direkt in die Taschen der Goslarer Bürger. Die Stadt blühte auf. Schon 1281 gehörte sie der Hanse fest an, deren Mitbegründerin sie war.

Das Verhängnis erreichte die Stadt 1552, als der Braunschweiger Herzog ihr den Rammelsberg und die Forsten abnahm.

Nach reichen Jahrzehnten im 15. und 16. Jahrhundert verlor Goslar zunehmend an Bedeutung.

The mines and the substantial profits from the smelters were the basis for Goslar's development into a populous city with six parish districts. More and more often emperors and kings came to stay the imperial palace, which was lavishly extended and furnished. At the same time the city was carefully designed according to plans laid down by St. Augustine. A "cross of churches" divided the town into sectors, and numerous abbeys and chapels crowned the surrounding hills. In the end emperor Heinrich III and his son Heinrich IV, who was born in Goslar, returned so often to the palace at Goslar that it was almost like a permanent residence. Important imperial diets were held here, and in 1056 the pope Victor II himself came to visit the emperor at Goslar.

During the imperial diets of the Salian and Hohenstaufen emperors at the Goslar palace European history was made.

But when their days ended, Goslar's heydays were over. While later emperors did not entirely forget the city, Wilhelm of Holland visited the palace once again in 1252/53, it ceased to be the navel of the Reich. Seeing themselves as the heirs of the earlier powers a few Patrician families and the large independent abbeys took over.

From now on the profits gained from mountains and woods found their way directly into the pockets of Goslar's citizens. The city prospered, and by 1281 it was a member of the Hanse whose co-founder it was.

Doom approached the city in 1552 when the feud with the Duke of Brunswick ended in the loss of the Rammelsberg mines and the forests.

With the rich decades of the 15th and 16th century over, Goslar step by step fell into oblivion.

Eingebettet in den Kranz der Harzberge liegt die alte Stadt. Die Wälder reichen dicht an die Wohnbebauung heran.

Seite 12/13: Über der bürgerlichen Stadt thront am Fuße der Berge der Saalbau der Kaiserpfalz.

The Harz mountains look down on the old city snuggling at their feet with the eaves of their forests almost touching the outlying houses.

Page 12/13: Below green mountains the great hall of the imperial palace towers above the city.

Neu- und Ersatzbauten konnten kaum noch errichtet werden. So hat die Altstadt über Jahrhunderte hinweg ihr bauliches Erbe bewahren können, denn "Armut erhält, Reichtum zerstört". Mit circa 100 ha Größe und etwa 1.800 Fachwerkhäusern im Rund der Befestigungsanlagen besitzt Goslar die größte zusammenhängend bebaute Altstadt in Deutschland. Und diese Altstadt wird von den Goslarern gehegt und gepflegt. Die historische Bausubstanz ist sorgsam modernisiert und bewohnt. So ist Goslars Altstadt lebendig - kein Museum.

Funds to repair buildings were few and money to build anew was even scarcer. So the old city retained its architectural heritage virtually unchanged, proving the old saw that "poverty maintains, but wealth destroys". With an area of about 100 hectares (250 acres) and some 1.800 half-timbered buildings, Goslar has the largest coherent old city in Germany. And this old city is cherished by its citizens. Carefully modernised to fit today's needs, the old houses are loved and lived in. This city is alive - not a dead museum.

Die Kaiserpfalz

Der Name Pfalz leitet sich vom lateinischen palatium ab und lebt bis heute in dem Wort Palast weiter. Im Heiligen Römischen Reich Deutscher Nation gab es viele Pfalzen als Unterkunftsorte für den Kaiser auf seinen Reisen, aber nur wenige waren wie Goslar Reichstagspfalzen. Bis heute ist der große Saal erhalten geblieben, in dem sich einst die Großen des Reiches zu Beratungen versammelt haben. Um 1050 erbaut, vielfach renoviert, aber immer genutzt, ist die "aula regis" ein stolzes Beispiel für die mittelalterliche Pracht des Kaisertums.

Die Wohngemächer der Herrscher waren winzig im Vergleich zu dem Saalbau. Von besonderer Bedeutung ist noch die Pfalzkapelle St. Ulrich. Es ist eine zweigeschossige sogenannte Doppelkapelle, in der im Erdgeschoß die Priester die Messe lasen, im Obergeschoß der Kaiser seinen Platz hatte und durch eine Deckenöffnung zum Altar blicken konnte. Das Erdgeschoß entspricht in seinem Grundriß einem griechischen Kreuz, das Obergeschoß ist dagegen achteckig und damit ein Symbol des Kaisertums. (Mehrere Pfalzkapellen und auch die Kaiserkrone sind achteckig.)

Vor seinem Tod 1056 hatte Kaiser Heinrich III. bestimmt, daß sein Leib in die Erbgruft nach Speyer überführt werden, sein Herz aber in Goslar verbleiben sollte. Hier hätte er am liebsten verweilt. Deshalb wurde sein Herz in einer achteckigen Kapsel zunächst im Goslarer Dom beigesetzt, nach dessen Abriß 1819 in die Ulrichskapelle gebracht und in einen Sarkophag eingefügt. Darüber liegt die Grabplatte aus dem 13. Jahrhundert mit dem Bild des bedeutendsten Salierkaisers, in dessen Regierungszeit noch die Einheit des Abendlandes bestand, die dann unter seinem in

The Imperial Palace

The German word Pfalz is derived from the Latin palatium, still alive in German 'Palast' and English 'palace'. There were many such palaces in the Holy Roman Empire to host the emperors on their journeys through their empire, but only of few of them were places to hold imperial diets at. The great hall where the great of the Reich once gathered for their councils has survived until our days. Built around 1050, often repaired, but always in use, this aula regis (King's Hall) is a proud example of the splendours of the medieval empire.

In comparison, the living quarters of the emperors were small and insignificant. The other outstanding part of this palace is the chapel of St. Ulrich. It is a two-storeyed chapel. While a priest read mass on the ground floor, the emperor had his seat on the upper floor and viewed the altar through a hole in the ceiling. The layout of the floors differs: the ground floor is designed in the shape of a Greek cross while the upper floor has the shape of an octagon, and thus is symbolic of imperial rule. (A number of palace chapels throughout the country is octagonal, and so is the imperial crown:)

Before his death in 1056, emperor Heinrich III. had decreed that his body was to be laid to rest in the tomb of his house at Speyer, but his heart was to remain at Goslar since he had enjoyed staying there most. Accordingly his heart was buried in a octagonal capsule at the Goslar cathedral, and when this cathedral was torn down in 1819, the capsule was transferred to the Chapel of St. Ulrich and added to a sarcophagus. This is covered by a 13th century ledger showing an image of this important Salian emperor. During his reign the unity of the west was still preserved, but it was lost in

Die zweigeschossige Pfalzkapelle St. Ulrich (Mitte des 12. Jahrhunderts)

The two-storeyed palace chapel of St. Ulrich (mid 12th century)

15

Links: Unter der Grabplatte in der Ulrichskapelle ruht das Herz Kaiser Heinrichs III. († 1056).

Rechts: Die romanischen Lehnen des Kaiserstuhls im Gewölbe der Kaiserpfalz.

Goslar geborenen Sohn Heinrich IV. im Streit mit dem Papst zerbrach. Sein Bußgang nach Canossa war dafür ein Merkstein der Geschichte.

Vor dem Kaiserhaus stehen die Reiterstandbilder aus der Zeit um 1900. Friedrich Barbarossa war einer der bedeutendsten Kaiser, der hier vor seinem Kreuzzug ins Heilige Land, bei dem er tödlich verunglückte, seinen Streit mit dem Braunschweiger Herzog Heinrich dem Löwen beendete. Unter Kaiser Wilhelm I. wurde die Kaiserpfalz grundlegend renoviert und zum Nationaldenkmal hergerichtet.

Dazu gehörte auch die Ausmalung des Saales durch Prof. Wislicenus mit Historiengemälden in den beiden letzten Jahrzehnten des 19. Jahrhunderts. Sie schildern, eingebunden in

Left: Below this ledger in the Chapel of St. Ulrich rests the heart of the emperor Heinrich III. († 1056).

Right: The Romanesque backs of the Throne in the vaults of the Imperial Palace.

in the days of his son Heinrich IV, born in Goslar, whose feuds with the pope and pilgrimage to Canossa have become a marker in history.

The equestrian statues in front of the palace date from around 1900. Friedrich Barbarossa was one of the most important emperors. Before leaving for his fateful crusade to the Holy Land, on which he met his end, he settled his dispute with the Duke of Braunschweig (Brunswick) Heinrich dem Löwen. In the days of emperor Wilhelm I the palace was restored and made a national heritage site.

Part of that restoration where the murals in the great hall. Created by Professor Wislicenus in the 80s and 90s of last century and weaving a web of fact and fiction, these paintings tell of

Wandbilder in der „aula regis".
Links: Einzug Heinrich IV. in Mainz (1105).
Rechts: Wiedererstehung der alten Reichsherrlichkeiten (1871).

Murals in the aula "Regis".
Left: Heinrich IV. entering Mainz (1105).
Right: Revival of the ancient imperial glory (1871).

die Sagenwelt, wichtige Szenen aus der Geschichte der für Goslar bedeutenden Herrscher. Das große Mittel-bild zeigt eine Apotheose des Kaisertums.

Die insgesamt 67 Wandgemälde sind im typischen Stil der wilhelminischen Kaiserzeit gemalt, einem Stil, der dem heutigen Betrachter nur allzu schwülstig vorkommt. Gleichwohl haben die Bilder ihre historische Bedeutung. Eine aufwendige Restauration ist nötig, weil die Bilder zum Teil bis in die Substanz hinein gefährdet sind - insbesondere wegen der raumklimatischen Bedingungen. Und die sind sehr kompliziert - vor allem wegen der vielen Besucher, die sich alljährlich durch das historisch bedeutendste Bauwerk der Stadt führen lassen.

portant events in the lives of kings and emperors who influenced Goslar's place in history. The large painting in the centre shows an apotheosis of imperial rule.

All 67 murals were painted in a style quite typical for the Wilhelmine era. Today people tend to see this style of imperial days as much too bombastic to be pleasing. Nevertheless these paintings have their place in history. So after some one hundred years an extensive restoration is needed because many of the murals are in critical condition, not the least because of the difficult airing and ventilation conditions in the rooms, a tribute to the thousands of visitors who are being guided through the historically greatest house of the town each year.

Links: Der Thronsessel der Salier- und Hohenstaufenkaiser	*Left: The throne of the Salian and Hohenstaufen emperors*
Rechts: Ausstellung von Architekturteilen in der Domvorhalle	*Right: An exhibition of architectural remains in the cathedral's porch*
Seite 19: Die Domvorhalle	*Page 19: The porch of the cathedral*

Zum Pfalzbezirk gehörte auch der Goslarer Dom als Reichstift, von dem nach seinem Abbruch 1819 nur die Vorhalle erhalten geblieben ist.

As an independent imperial convent, the old Goslar cathedral was part of the palace district. Torn down in 1819, only the porch survived.

Der Dom zu Goslar | *The Cathedral at Goslar*

Rathaus und Marktplatz

Die Westseite des Marktplatzes begrenzt das in der Mitte des 15. Jahrhunderts erbaute Rathaus. Es enthält alle für die bürgerliche Gemeinschaft in jener Zeit notwendigen Räume: Im Keller die Gaststätte mit dem alleinigen Privileg, Wein ausschenken zu dürfen, den "Ratsweinkeller", im Erdgeschoß die Markthalle und darüber der große Saal, der wie eine heutige Stadthalle vielfältig genutzt werden konnte.

An der Rückseite befinden sich drei Räume für die damalige Verwaltung: das Zimmer des Schreibers mit dem Archiv, der Gerichtsraum und der "Huldigungssaal", der Sitzungsraum der Stadtväter. Dieser ist kurz nach 1500 vollständig vertäfelt und ausgemalt worden. An den Wänden verkünden die Sibyllen, die weissagenden Frauen der Antike, Kaisern ihre Orakelsprüche über einen künftigen Segenskaiser. Unter der Decke erklären Propheten und Evangelisten die in den Mittelbildern geschilderte Geschichte um die Menschwerdung Christi.

Vor der Front des Rathauses steht der mittelalterliche Pranger, und die Mitte des Strahlenpflasters betont der romanische Dreischalenbrunnen mit dem goldenen Reichsadler als Bekrönung. Dieser Adler ist im übrigen eine Kopie - das Original steht wohlverwahrt und geschützt im Rathaus. In der Vergangenheit ist es nämlich mehrfach vorgekommen, daß dem Kunstwerk die Flügel gerupft oder gar die Beine gebrochen wurden. Die beiden Bronzeschalen des Brunnens mit ihren Drachen und Löwenköpfen sind hingegen noch original.

Seite 21: Der Marktplatz

Seite 22/23: Der Huldigungssaal

Town Hall and Market-Place

The west side of the market square is dominated by the town hall. Built in the middle of the 15th century, the building houses all the public rooms needed for the social life of the day: in the cellar there was a pub, the only one with the privilege of serving wine ("the council's wine cellar"); the ground floor was taken up by the actual market hall, and the floor above featured a large multi-purpose hall quite similar to those today.

At the back there are three rooms for the former town administration: the office for the city scribe with the archives, the courtroom, and the "hall of homage", the assembly room of the town councillors. To underscore its particular importance, this last room had been panelled and painted with murals shortly after 1500. On the walls sibyls, those wise women of ancient days, offer the emperors their prophecies on a coming emperor of peace. And on the ceiling prophets and evangelists explain the incarnation of Christ depicted in the paintings in the centre.

A typical medieval pillory stands in front of the town hall, while the radiating pavement of the square focuses the visitor's eyes on the Romanesque fountain whose basins are crowned with the imperial eagle. This golden eagle, by the way, is only a copy. The original has long been kept safe at the town hall, for too often ruthless pranksters have damaged the bird's wings or even broken its legs. But the two bronze basins of the fountain with their dragons and lion heads are still the historic ones that have endured the centuries.

Page 21: The Market-Place

Page 22/23: The "Hall of Homage"

Die Worth, das Gildehaus der Fernhandelskaufleute am Markt.

The Worth, the guild hall of the merchants, borders the market square.

An der Südseite des Marktplatzes steht die Worth, das Gildehaus der Fernhandelskaufleute. Der Name erinnert daran, daß sich einst diese Händler einen trockenen Platz im Talgrund ausgesucht haben. In den Varianten Worth, Wurth, Warft, Wörth und Werder sind derartige Flurnamen für Bauplätze am Wasser in Deutschland weit verbreitet. Die Fernhandelskaufleute waren mit ihren selbstverwalteten Gemeinschaften, die Genossenschaften ähnelten, einst die Zellen für die Gründung bürgerlicher Städte. Deshalb bildeten sie auch die wichtigste Gilde in Goslar.

Ihrem Rang entsprechend ist auch ihr 1494 erbautes Haus gestaltet und reich verziert. Über der Kaufhalle unten befand sich einst im Obergeschoß ein großer Saal für Festlichkei-

The Worth, the guildhall of the im- and export merchants, has its place on the south side of the market square. The name keeps alive the fact that the merchants once chose a dry place down in the valley to set up business. Throughout Germany, variations of this name such as Worth, Wurth, Warft, Wörth, and Werder indicate a site near water. The im- and export merchants with their self-administered societies, in many ways the forerunners of today's co-operatives, once were the nuclei for the founding of independent cities. So this guild was dominant in Goslar, too.

The guild hall, built in 1494, is quite appropriate to the social rank of this guild. While the groundfloor housed the actual exchange, the upper storey once contained a large all for celebra-

Links: Das "Dukatenmännchen", ein humorvolles Rechtssymbol.

Rechts: Die Kaiser und das Wappen mit der Krone sind Zeichen der besonderen Stellung der Gilde.

Left:The "Dukatenmännchen" is a deftly humorous symbol of justice.

Right: The statues of the emperors and the coat of arms with the crown show the special status of the guild.

ten der Mitglieder. Von den Kaisern mit Freiheits- und Zollprivilegien bedacht, haben sie ihre Stellung durch die Ausstellung barocker Kaiserfiguren in gotischen Nischen demonstriert. Von diesen Figuren hatte der Spötter Heinrich Heine einmal behauptet, sie sähen aus "wie gebratene Universitätspedelle". Ein Rechtssymbol besonderer Art ist auch das "Dukatenmännchen" an der Ostecke, das drastisch die Strafe darstellt, die den erwartete, der seine Schulden nicht bezahlen konnte. Als Zeichen ihrer bevorrechtigten Stellung im Reich führten die Goslarer Fernhandelskaufleute die Königskrone in ihrem Gildewappen.

tions of its members. The liberties and custom privileges granted to them by the emperors prompted the guild to put up those Baroque statues of emperors in their Gothic niches. Heinrich Heine, the German writer so well known for his biting wit and sarcasm, once said of those statues that they looked "like fried university janitors". The "ducat manikin" at the eastern corner of the building is a symbol of a rather strange justice illustrating the punishment facing those who could not repay their debt. Also adorning the building is the guild's coat of arms, which carries the crown in it to underline the privileged position Goslar's merchants enjoyed.

Das Glockenspiel am Markt zeigt im Figurenlauf die Geschichte des Bergbaus in Goslar.

In its procession of figures, the carillon at the market square tells the history of mining at Goslar.

1968 konnte in einem großen Bergdankfest unter der Beteiligung von Knappenabordnungen aus ganz Europa die tausendjährige Betriebsdauer des Bergbaus im Rammelsberg gefeiert werden. Aus diesem Anlaß stiftete die Preussag als Eigentümerin der Gruben ein Glockenspiel. In dem Figurenumlauf wird die Technikgeschichte des Erzabbaus in vier Gruppen geschildert. Viermal täglich laufen die Figuren aus dem barocken Haus gegenüber vom Rathaus, zu anderen Zeiten erklingen nur die Bronzeglocken, deren Speise aus dem Erz des Rammelsberges erschmolzen wurde. Zu Zeiten des Figurenumlaufes ist auf dem Marktplatz oftmals kaum noch ein Plätzchen zu ergattern.

1968 was the year of endless celebrations as miners' delegations from all over Europe paid homage to one-thousand years of continuous mining at and in the Rammelsberg mountain. On this special occasion the Preussag, then the owner and operator of the mines, donated the carillon housed in the upper storey of the Baroque house opposite the town hall. Accompanied by the music, sets of figures help to illustrate the technical side of mining history. The complete presentation takes place four times a day. At other times only the bronze bells are clanged, bells cast from metal ore that was once mined here. As tourists and locals alike enjoy this old-fashioned ritual, standing space is hard to find at carillon hours.

Das Bäckergildehaus von 1501/1557 | *The bakers' guild hall of 1501/1557*

Gildehäuser

Die Zeit um 1500 ist ein Höhepunkt des Bürgertums. Die Gewinne aus Bergbau und Hüttenwesen führten zu vielen Neubauten. Als Beispiele dafür seien hier das Bäckergildehaus und das Brusttuch erwähnt. Von den sieben Gildehäusern stammen nur die Worth und die Häuser der Bäcker und Münzer aus dieser Zeit, die anderen mußten nach dem Stadtbrand von 1780 neu erbaut werden.

Das Brusttuch wurde 1521 von dem aus einer Patrizierfamilie stammenden Meister Thilling erbaut. Wegen seines reichen Schnitzwerks am Fachwerkobergeschoß, in dem das humanistische Weltbild jener Zeit vorgestellt wird, verdient es besondere Beachtung. Auf einer Dachknagge ist das zweite humorvolle Wahrzeichen Goslars, die Butterhanne, zu finden.

Guild Halls

The years around 1500 were the first heydays of an emerging middle class. The profits from the mines and the smelters made numerous new buildings possible. Two prominent examples of this period are the bakers' guild hall and the "Brusttuch". Of the seven guild halls, only the "Worth" and the bakers' and minters' halls survived the great fire of 1780. The others had to be rebuilt then.

The "Brusttuch" was built in 1521 by Master Thilling, who came from one of Goslar's patrician families. The rich carvings of the timbers of the upper storey provide impressive insights into the life of those days and the humanistic views of the world that prevailed then. Here Goslar's second humorous landmark, the Butterhanne, is found at the end of a roof beam.

Der Braunschweiger Bildschnitzer Simon Stappen hat das Fachwerkobergeschoß des 1521 erbauten Hauses erst fünf Jahre später mit dem Figurenschmuck versehen. In der Zwischenzeit hatte der gelehrte Bauherr und Magister mit der Abzahlung seiner Schulden zu kämpfen. Mit dem Schnitzwerk wollte er den Betrachtern vermutlich sein akademisches Wissen demonstrieren, denn dort stehen zwischen den Fenstern die antiken Götterfiguren, die in jener Zeit eine vielfältige Bedeutung hatten. Sie verkörperten die wichtigsten Metalle anstelle der noch nicht erfundenen chemischen Kürzel, sie bestimmten zusammen mit den Tierkreiszeichen den gestirnten Himmel und damit zugleich im Sinne der Astrologie die Eigenschaften der Menschen, die in dem jeweiligen Zeichen geboren sind.

In humorvoller Weise hat der Schnitzer diese Gelehrtenwelt durch allerlei Fabelwesen und charakteristische Szenen miteinander verknüpft. Auch Anspielungen auf den Hausherren fehlen nicht, wenn zum Beispiel neben dem Erker Affen um Geld streiten oder an der Ecke der Bruder des Dukatenmännchens hockt. Er selbst tritt auf einer Knagge als Hüttenherr mit einem Blasebalg in der Hand auf, mit dem er seine Magd, die Butterhanne, auf den abwehrend entblößten Hintern pustet.

Die Ausmalung der Innenräume des Hauses erfolgte 1875 durch Professor Hermann Schaper aus Hannover. In dem bekanntesten Patrizierhaus der Stadt Goslar, das sich inzwischen zu einem der beliebtesten Fotomotive in der Innenstadt entwickelt hat, ist heute ein Hotel untergebracht. Dazu gehört auch ein stilvolles Restaurant, dessen ungewöhnliche Einrichtung und Architektur in der Stadt ihresgleichen suchen dürften.

Simon Stappen, a wood carver from Braunschweig (Brunswick) was commissioned to do the decorative carvings. But although the house itself was erected in 1521, these carvings were not completed until five years later because the erudite owner and master had a hard time repaying his debt. The carvings were probably intended to demonstrate the owner's academic knowledge. There are, for example, images of the ancient Gods and Goddesses between the windows, figures that among other meanings were the symbols for the most important metals in an age that had not yet arrived at the periodic system. At the same time these gods were part of the starry night sky. Together with the zodiacs they were said to determine the character traits and talents of people born under a given sign.

The wood carver must have enjoyed his commission. For the presentation of this world of knowledge is interspersed with images of fabulous beasts and other characteristic scenes. The monkeys quarrelling over money beside the oriel, or the twin brother to the Worth's ducat mannequin squatting in a corner are obvious puns at his employer, who is depicted himself at the end of one of the beams in the role of a mine owner approaching his maid, the Butterhanne, with bellows in his hands.

Following the trends of the day, the house was painted and newly decorated inside by professor Hermann Schaper from Hanover in 1875. Over the years the Brusttuch has become Goslar's best-known and most photographed patrician house in the city centre. Converted into a hotel, it also houses a very stylish restaurant whose unusual furnishing and architecture are unparalleled even in a town such as Goslar.

Das "Brusttuch", wohl das schönste mittelalterliche Patrizierhaus Goslars.

The "Brusttuch" may be Goslar's most impressive medieval patrician house.

Links: Mittelschiff und Altarraum der Marktkirche SS. Cosmas und Damian.

Rechts: Die Taufkapelle mit dem 1573 von Magnus Karsten gegossenen Messingbecken.

Seite 31: Die Marktkirche

Left: Nave and chancel of the Market Church SS. Cosmas and Damian.

Right: The christening chapel with the brass font cast by Magnus Karsten in 1573.

Page 31: The Market Church

Die Kirchen

47 Kirchen, Klöster und Kapellen besaß Goslar um 1500. Sie hatten ein vergleichbares Schicksal: in romanischer Zeit erbaut, in der Gotik erweitert, nach der Reformation (1528), soweit sie nicht mehr für die Gemeinden gebraucht wurden, zu Wohnungen umgebaut oder abgebrochen. Die fünf Pfarrkirchen sind nach dem Vorbild des Goslarer Domes als große Basiliken mit zweitürmigen Westwerken errichtet worden. Alle besitzen eine reiche Ausstattung. In der Marktkirche gehören dazu die romanischen

The Churches

There were 47 churches, abbeys and chapels in Goslar around 1500, and the fate of most of them is quite similar: they were built in the days of Romanesque style, extended during the Gothic period, and fell into disuse after the Reformation (1528). With the exception of the parish churches they were either turned into homes or demolished. Goslar's five parish churches followed the design of the cathedral, large basilicas with two towering belfries. All are richly furnished. One of the treasures of the

Glasmalereien. Beachtenswert sind auch die 1991 geschaffenen modernen abstrakten, in ihrer Farbgebung eindrucksvollen Chorfenster von Johannes Schreiter, einem der bekanntesten Glasmaler unserer Zeit.

Den Nordturm bekrönt die Türmerstube für den Nacht- und Feuerwächter. Die unterschiedliche Gestalt der zwei Türme entstand nach 1573, als ein Brand sie beschädigte. Nach einem weiteren Brand 1844 wurden die Türme noch einmal erneuert.

Stadtbrände vernichteten 1728 und 1780 große Teile der Unterstadt. Der Wiederaufbau durch schlichte Fachwerkbauten war eine beachtliche Leistung. Für den barocken Neubau der Stephanikirche kamen Spenden aus dem gesamten norddeutschen Raum in die Stadt. Nach wenigen Jahren waren so die Lücken, wenn auch mit bescheideneren Häusern, wieder geschlossen.

1732 konnte die Pfarrkirche geweiht werden. Mit ihrem die Häuser hoch überragenden Turm ist sie die einzige von Daniel Köppel im schlichten norddeutschen Barock errichtete Kirche in Goslar.

Die Hallenkirche besitzt, wie in jener Zeit üblich, an der Nordseite eine große Empore, um alle Gemeindemitglieder unterbringen zu können. Zu den Ausstattungsstücken gehören ein großer Rokokoaltar und eine Kanzel aus derselben Zeit. Die stark plastisch geschnitzte Brüstung der Orgelempore stammt aus dem aufgelassenen Kloster Riechenberg, aus dem weitere Barockaltäre in die Pfarrkirche St. Jakobi gelangt sind. Sie lassen Rückschlüsse auf die Pracht der Ausstattung der nur noch als Ruine erhaltenen romanischen Klosterkirche nördlich von Goslar zu.

Market Church are its Romanesque stained glass windows. A stark and yet fascinating contrast to them are the modern stained glass windows of the apse, created by the well-known artist Johannes Schreiter in 1991.

The northern tower of the Market Church houses the quarters of the night- and fire-watchers. The different shape of the two towers is due repairs after the fire of 1573. Damages caused by another fire in 1844 made further restorations necessary.

Two great fires in 1728 and 1780 destroyed most of the lower section of the town. Rebuilding it with half-timbered houses of a yet simpler style was an amazing feat for those hard times. The new Baroque building of the parish church of St. Stephanus was made possible by donations from all over northern Germany. In this way, most of the damages had been repaired within a few years.

Designed by the architect Daniel Köppel, the new parish church was consecrated in 1732. With its single belfry towering over the lower town, it is Goslar's only church built in the simple style of Northgerman Baroque.

Typical for the parish churches of the time, it has a large gallery at the northern end to accommodate all parishioners. Among its furnishings are a large Rococo altar and a pulpit from the same period. The extensively carved railing of the organ gallery has been taken from the former abbey of Riechenberg. Further Baroque altars from that abbey are to be found at the parish church of St. Jacob. In these and other fascinating pieces the memory of the past splendour of this Romanesque abbey at Riechenberg lives on, whose ruins are found north of Goslar.

Hoch überragt die barocke Stephani-kirche die Häuser der Unterstadt.

The Baroque Stephanikirche towers high above the lower town.

Links: Die Marienklage des Meisters Hans Witten von etwa 1515.

Rechts: Blick auf den Altar in der Jakobikirche.

Left: The pieta by the master artisan Hans Witten, about 1515.

Right: View to the altar of the Church of St. Jakobi.

Die Pfarrkirche St. Jakobi steckt voller Gegensätze. Sie ist an sich die älteste, doch aus dem 11. Jahrhundert ist nur ein Teil des wuchtigen Westwerks erhalten. Danach hat fast jede Generation etwas verändert oder hinzugefügt. In dieser Kirche wurde 1527 zuerst die Reformation in Goslar eingeführt - heute ist sie die einzige katholische Kirche der Altstadt. Als das leerstehende Gotteshaus 1802 der damals sehr kleinen katholischen Gemeinde zur Verfügung gestellt wurde, holten sich die Mitglieder aus aufgelassenen Klöstern die Ausstattungsstücke. Darunter befinden sich kostbare Stücke wie z. B. die frühbarocke Orgel und die lebensgroße Holzfigur der Marienklage (Pieta) des Meisters Hans Witten von etwa 1515, sowie ein Bronzetaufbecken und ein überlebensgroßes Triumphkreuz (um 1500).

The parish church of St. Jacob's is full of contradictions. Basically it is the oldest church of the town, but only parts of the massive west works from the 11th century have survived. Almost every generation has added to or changed the building and its style. It was here that the Reformation was first introduced in Goslar in 1527 - and today it is the only Catholic church in the old town. When the empty church was turned over to the very small Catholic congregation in 1802, its members collected the necessary furnishings from the secularised abbeys of the area. Among the treasures that thus found their way to this church are the organ of early Baroque vintage, the life-size pieta by master artisan Hans Witten of 1515, a bronze baptismal font and a larger than life crucifix (about 1500).

Die Pfarrkirche St. Jakobi, die einzige katholische Kirche der Altstadt.

The parish church of St. Jacob's, the only Catholic church of the old town.

35

Die Kirche des ehemaligen Nonnenklosters Neuwerk ist ein Musterbeispiel romanischer Baukunst. Seit der Weihe 1186 ist sie fast unverändert erhalten geblieben. Die dreischiffige, kreuzförmige Basilika mit zweitürmigem Westwerk besitzt reichen Steinmetzschmuck, unter dem henkelartige Ösen am Chor und innen an den Diensten der Pfeiler originell auffallen. Die Henkel an den Diensten unterbrechen den Weg zum Weltenrichter in der Spitze des westlichen Gurtbogens. Sie zeigen auf der Südseite Symbole des Bösen und an der Nordseite des Christentums. Als Baumeister nennt sich unter einer Engelsfigur an der inneren Südwand des Mittelschiffes der Steinmetz Wilhelmus.

Im Chorraum haben sich romanische Fresken erhalten. In dreistufigem Aufbau zeigen sie am Sockel Christus zwischen Königen und Aposteln, darüber die alttestamentarischen Szenen der Opferung Isaaks und Jephtas Tochter. Außen links findet sich Jakobs Traum von der Himmelsleiter und rechts Judith mit dem Haupt des Holofernes, dazu in der Wölbung die Himmelskönigin auf dem Thron der Weisheit. Auf dem Schildbogen darüber breitet Christus segnend die Arme aus, und im Kreuzgewölbe des Chores öffnet sich der Blick in den von Heiligen bevölkerten Himmel.

Der ursprünglich den Chorraum zum Mittelschiff hin abschließende Lettner aus der Zeit um 1230 ist umgesetzt worden und dient heute als Orgelempore. Die Lettnerkanzel schmückt auf der Vorderseite die Figurengruppe "Christus überreicht seiner Mutter die Himmelskrone." Rechts und links stehen die Apostelfürsten Petrus und Paulus sowie zwei weitere Apostel. Es sind Gipshalbreliefs in einer im Harzraum häufigen, sonst in romanischer Zeit selten verwendeten Technik.

The former convent church of Neuwerk is a masterpiece of Romanesque style. Consecrated in 1186 it has survived the storms of time virtually unchanged. Built as typical basilica with nave, aisles and transept and two towering spires, it features rich and unusual masonry. An example for this are the strange, handle-like eyelets at the choir and on the inside of the arch supports, which interrupt the way to the world's judge in the top of the western arch. On the south side they show symbols of evil, and on the north side symbols of Christianity. According to an inscription beneath the figure of an angel on the inner south wall of the nave mason Wilhelmus has been their maker.

Romanesque frescos have survived in the apse. Arranged in three levels, they show on the bottom line Jesus Christ among kings and apostles, above scenes from the old testament - the sacrifice of Isaac and Jephta's daughter. To the left there is an image of Jacob's ladder, and to the right there is Judith with the head of Holofernes. The vault above shows the Queen of Heaven on the throne of wisdom. On the arch above, Jesus Christ is depicted, arms spread wide in blessing, and the painted vaulting of the choir opens a view into a heaven peopled by saints.

The rood-screen of 1230 that originally separated nave and chancel has been moved to its present position to serve as organ gallery. The pulpit of the rood-screen shows a set of sculptures called "Christ hands his mother the crown of heaven". To the left and right there are the apostles Peter and Paul and two minor apostles. These half-reliefs have been done in plaster, a sculpturing technique common to the Harz but rare elsewhere in the Romanesque period.

Der Chor der Klosterkirche Neuwerk mit den romanischen Wandmalereien.

The apse of the convent church Neuwerk with its Romanesque frescos.

Links: Kanzel, Empore, Orgelprospekt und Altar sind Schnitzwerk der Familie Lessen um 1700.

Rechts: Das romanische Mittelschiff mit der Empore unter dem Westwerk.

Wie eine Burg des Glaubens thront über der Stadt die Kirche auf dem Frankenberg. Die einheimischen Sachsen hatten die ersten nach hier geholten Facharbeiter, die die Gruben im Rammelsberg betreiben sollten, "Franken" genannt. Der Name blieb an ihrem Gotteshaus haften und bis heute ist es die Pfarrkirche der Bergleute geblieben. Der romanische Bau hat seine zwei Westtürme verloren und dafür eine barocke Haube erhalten. Die Innenausstattung schuf die bedeutende Goslarer Bildschnitzerfamilie Lessen in der Zeit um 1700. Sie bestimmt mit dem Hochaltar, der Kanzel, der Bergmannsempore und der Orgel den Ostteil des Kirchenraumes. Unter den Türmen ist im Westen die Herrscherempore erhalten geblieben, deren Säulen romanischen Steinmetzschmuck besitzen.

Left: The carved pulpit, gallery, organ front and altar were all created by the famous Lessen family around 1700.

Right: The Romanesque nave with the gallery beneath the west works.

The church on the Frankenberg towers above the city like a fortress of Christian faith. "Franks" had been the name for the first tradesmen, the native Saxons had brought in to run their mines at the Rammelsberg. And that name also went with their church. Until today, this church has remained the parish church of the miners. in the course of times the Romanesque building lost its two tours and got a Baroque steeple instead. Most of its interior has been created by Goslar's famous family of wood carvers, Lessen, around 1700. These works together with the high altar, the pulpit, the miners' gallery and the organ dominate the eastern section of the church. In the western section the king's gallery beneath the former towers has survived, its piers being decorated by Romanesque masonry.

Die Pfarrkirche SS. Peter und Paul auf dem Frankenberg.

The parish church of SS. Peter and Paul on the Frankenberg.

Das Kleine Heilige Kreuz und das Küsterhaus auf dem Frankenberg.

The Kleine Heilige Kreuz and the sexton's house on the Frankenberg.

Die Hospitäler

Fünf mittelalterliche Hospitäler sind in Goslar erhalten geblieben, davon dienen drei noch kirchlichen Zwecken. Ihre Bezeichnung ist von lateinisch "hospes" = Gast abgeleitet. Die Häuser waren Sozialstationen, in denen die Alten und Schwachen der Gemeinde aufgenommen wurden, wenn sie keine häusliche Pflege fanden. Am Frankenberger Plan ist der kirch-

The Hospitals

Five of the medieval hospitals have survived in Goslar, and of these three are still being used by the church. The word "hospital" is derived from the Latin "hospes" = guest, and accordingly these houses served as charity institutions, hosting the old and the weak of the parish when no help at home could be found. At the Frankenberger Plan this religious context is

40

Links: Der Frankenberger Plan mit seinem Brunnen.

Rechts: Das Tor von 1510 am Aufgang zum barocken Kloster Frankenberg.

Left: the Frankenberger Plan with its fountain.

Right: The portal of 1510 marks the approach to the Baroque convent on the Frankenberg.

liche Zusammenhang noch gut abzulesen, weil hier, von außen an die hohe Friedhofsmauer angelehnt, das Pfarrhaus, das Küsterhaus von 1504, das Hospital (14. Jahrhundert) und das Pfarrwitwenhaus nebeneinander stehen.

Das Küsterhaus bildet zugleich den Zugang zum Friedhof und den zur Kirche vom Frankenberger Plan aus. Es besitzt die älteste Datierung eines Fachwerkhauses in Goslar und nennt den Altar St. Thomas in der Kirche, zu dessen Ausstattung es gehörte.

Das mit reichem Steinmetzschmuck versehene Portal von 1510 führt zum ehemaligen Magdaleniterinnenkloster auf dem Frankenberg. Der stattliche Barockbau dient heute als kirchliches Alten- und Pflegeheim.

Der Brunnen ist eine Schöpfung von Professor Fürstenberg (um 1950) unter Verwendung einer älteren Schale.

still most obvious. Leaning against the outside of the high walls of the churchyard, the parsonage, the sexton's house of 1504, the hospital (14th century), and the house for the parson's widow stand neighbourly side by side.

The graveyard and the church are entered from the Frankenberger Plan by way of the sexton's house. Dated by its inscriptions, it is one of the oldest half-timbered buildings in Goslar. The inscriptions name the altar of St. Thomas at the church as the owner.

Rich stone-cuttings adorn the portal of 1510 which leads to the former convent of St. Magdalene on the Frankenberg. Today this impressive Baroque building serves as an old people's and nursing home of the church.

The fountain on the Frankenberger Plan has been created around 1950 by professor Fürstenberg, making use of an older basin.

Das Hospital Großes Heiliges Kreuz am Hohen Weg im Pfalzbezirk.

The Hospital Großes Heiliges Kreuz at the Hoher Weg in the palace district.

Das Große Heilige Kreuz ist vermutlich das älteste bürgerliche Hospital in Deutschland. Im Jahre 1254 wurde es vom Rat der Stadt als Konkurrenzunternehmen für das gegenüberliegende Hospital der Deutschordensritter begründet, das es schließlich auch verdrängt hat. Benutzt wurde für den Bau das Grundstück eines Adligen, dessen Wohnturm - eine Kemenate - erhalten geblieben ist. Sie steht als gutes Beispiel für die romanische Baukunst neben dem Einfahrtstor. Mit Altenwohnungen dient das Gebäude noch teilweise dem ursprünglichen Zweck; in der Däle haben Kunsthandwerker ihre Stände. Im Erdgeschoß hält die kleine St. Johanneskapelle die kirchliche Tradition aufrecht. Im Obergeschoß befindet sich die Erinnerungsstätte des Goslarer Jägerbataillons.

The Großes Heiliges Kreuz may well be the oldest secular hospital of Germany. It was founded in 1254 by the town council as a competitor to the hospital of the Deutschordensritter (Teutonic Order) across the street, which it eventually replaced. The site of this hospital had once belonged to a nobleman whose living quarters, a kemenate (bower) still remains. Being a good example of Romanesque architecture it is found right beside the entrance gate. A number of the rooms have been restored to their original use, serving as apartments to old people. Artisans of the most different fields have their stalls in the entrance hall. The tradition of the church is upheld by the small chapel of St. John, while more recent memories are revived by a memorial to the battalion of Goslar infantry.

Das Hospital St. Annen in der Unter-stadt an der Glockengießerstraße.

The hospital of St. Annen in the Glockengießerstraße in the lower town.

Besonders idyllisch liegt das im 15. Jahrhundert errichtete Hospital St. Annen in der Stephanigemeinde der Unterstadt. Ein Fachwerkbürgerhaus mit den Resten einer romanischen Kemenate wurde damals dafür verwendet. Die Däle ist heute der Kapellenraum, dessen Ausstattung mit Kunstwerken von der Romanik bis zum Barock ein stimmungsvolles Ensemble bildet. Hervorzuheben sind hier drei romanische Vortragekreuze - das älteste über dem Eingang der Schranke, spätgotische Schnitzfiguren aus verlorenen Altarschreinen, Reste von Glasmalereien und die gestickte Decke mit Darstellungen aus der Margaretenlegende. Zum überwiegend barocken Inventar gehören der vom Bildschnitzer Lessen gestiftete Altar, die Wappenscheiben und die Wand- und Deckenmalereien.

Built in the 15th century, the hospital of St. Annen has certainly been erected at a rather cosy spot. It was converted from a half-timbered home that incorporated the remains of an older Romanesque bower. The old main hall today is used as the chapel, whose natural make-up and rich collection of pieces of art from the Romanesque to the Baroque blend into a mellow ensemble. The three Romanesque crucifixes - the oldest is found above the entrance - deserve as much attention as the late Gothic figures from long lost altar shrines, some remains of stained glass windows, and last not least the embroidered tapestry showing the legend of St. Margaret. The Baroque altar of St. Annen was donated by Goslar's master carver Lessen. Coats of arms, painted walls and ceiling complete it.

Der Innenraum des St. Annenhauses an der Glockengießerstraße.

Inside the Hospital of St. Annen in the Glockengießerstraße.

Das *"Runenhaus" an der Gosestraße. Die eingeschnitzten Marken sind Meisterzeichen der Tuchmacher und Walker.*

The House of Runes in the Gosestraße. The carvings are the trademarks of the master clothmakers and fullers.

Die Bürgerhäuser

Staunend wandern heute Menschen aus nah und fern durch die engen Gassen, an deren Seiten sich die Fachwerkhäuser reihen. Dennoch ist die Stadt kein Freilichtmuseum. Die Bauten sind nach Kräften modernisiert und bewohnt. So leben mit rund 12.000 Einwohnern derzeit etwa genauso viele Bürger in der Altstadt wie im Mittelalter.

Diese Altstadt ist auch weit größer als man es zunächst vermutet. Zusammen mit dem Ring der mittelalterlichen Befestigungsanlagen umfaßt sie rund 100 Hektar! Mehr als 1500 der Bürgerhäuser sind Fachwerkbauten in den verschiedenen Stilformen seit Ausgang des Mittelalters.

The Patrician Houses

Filled with awe and admiration visitors from all parts of the world today walk the narrow alleys lined with old half-timbered houses. Yet the town is not an open air museum. All these houses are constantly lived in. Carefully modernised, they provide room for some 12.000 people. This is about the same number of citizens that lived in the old medieval town.

This old town is certainly larger than the visitor initially expects it to be. Together with its surrounding ring of fortifications it covers an area of about 100 hectares (about 250 acres) with more than 1500 half-timbered buildings representing the different styles since the Middle Ages.

Die Bergstraße mit dem Stammhaus der Familie Siemens.

The Bergstraße with the family seat of the Siemens family.

Der Verlust der Erträge aus dem Rammelsberger Bergbau und den Hütten im Jahre 1552 war für die Bevölkerung schwerwiegend. Die Armutsperiode hatte für uns Heutige jedoch auch gute Seiten. Die Bautätigkeit erlahmte. Die alten Häuser wurden mühsam erhalten, und somit können wir uns noch immer an dem mittelalterlichen Stadtbild erfreuen. Armut erhält, Reichtum zerstört durch Protz und Prunk! So blieben auch die Folgen der beiden großen Brandkatastrophen, die 1728 und 1780 die Unterstadt mit der Pfarrkirche St. Stephani vernichteten, für das Stadtbild unbedeutend.

Es gab aber auch noch Bauherren, die stattliche Fachwerkhäuser errich-

The loss of the profits from the Rammelsberg mines and the smelters in 1552 was a bitter burden for the people. But the long years of hardship and poverty of our ancestors has turned into an advantage for us today. Building activities came to an end, and it was with great difficulty that the existing houses were kept up. So the unbroken medieval townscape we enjoy today is a direct result of those bad times: poverty preserves, but wealth destroys by its need for pomp. Even the great fires of 1728 and 1780 that destroyed the lower town and its parish church of St. Stephen had little effect on the townscape.

But even in those days there were still some people who could afford to build

Links: Der Skulpturengarten des Mönchehaus-Museums, des Zentrums Moderne Kunst in Goslar.

Rechts: Im Mönchehaus-Garten, „Microbe" von Kaiserringträger Max Ernst (1974).

Left: The Sculpture Garden of the Mönchehaus Museum, center of modern art at Goslar.

Right: The "Microbe" by Kaiser Ring Recipient Max Ernst (1974) in the garden of the Mönchehaus.

ten konnten. Das größte wurde 1693 von Hans Siemens, dem Stammvater der weltberühmten Familie von Siemens, an der Bergstraße erbaut.

In einigen der historischen Bürgerhäuser sind Museen eingerichtet. Im 1528 erbauten und gut erhaltenen Mönchehaus residiert der Verein für moderne Kunst mit seinen Sammlungen. Internationale Künstler, die mit dem Goslarer Kaiserring ausgezeichnet wurden, stellen hier ihre Werke aus, darunter Henry Moore, Victor Vasarely und Joseph Beuys.

Es ist eine reizvolle Situation, in den mittelalterlichen, vom Gitter des Fachwerks geprägten Räumlichkeiten mit den Schöpfungen heute lebender Künstler konfrontiert zu werden.

impressive half-timbered houses. One of the largest in the Bergstraße was built in 1693 by Hans Siemens, the founder of this world famous dynasty.

Some of the historic patrician houses have been turned into museums. The well-preserved Mönchehaus of 1528 today is the home of the Society for Modern Art and its collections. The works of international artists who have received the Goslar Kaiserring Award are on display here, among them Henry Moore, Victor Vasarely, and Joseph Beuys.

It is a thrilling experience to confront the creations of the artists of today in a medieval ambience dominated by the grid of light and shadow of old half-timbered structures.

Das "Mönchehaus" von 1528, heute Museum für moderne Kunst.

The "Mönchehaus" of 1528 today is home to the Museum of Modern Art.

Links: Die Bergkanne von 1477 aus dem Goslarer Ratssilber.

Rechts: Die Geburt Christi, romanische Glasmalerei aus dem Goslarer Dom.

Left: The Bergkanne of 1477, a silver pitcher from the Goslar city treasure.

Right: The birth of Jesus Christ, a Romanesque stained glass window from the Goslar cathedral.

Das Goslarer Museum

Die Domherren wohnten einst nicht in der klösterlichen Gemeinschaft, sondern in stattlichen Häusern, verteilt im Pfalzbezirk. In eine derartige, 1574 errichtete Domkurie ist das Goslarer Museum eingezogen. Es zeigt in seinen Schätzen die Zeugen einer bürgerlichen Kultur aus sechs Jahrhunderten. Dazu gehören Kunstwerke und Gegenstände des Rates, der Gilden und der Patrizier.

Besondere Beachtung finden das Münzkabinett mit den Goslarer Prägungen, sowie der Domraum mit den beim Abbruch 1819 geretteten Ausstellungsstücken. Die Stirnwand wird von einer überlebensgroßen Triumphkreuzgruppe von 1520 beherrscht, die einst im Dom über dem Lettner den Bogen bis zum Gewölbe gefüllt hat.

The Goslar Museum

The canons of the cathedral did not live in a monastic community, they preferred the life in stately homes spread over the palace district. One of these, built in 1574, today houses Goslar's town museum. Its collections show the treasures of six centuries of bourgeois city life, among them pieces of art and every day utensils of the town council, the guilds, and the patricians.

Special attractions are the exhibits on the Goslar mint with its collection of local coins and the so-called cathedral room. Among the pieces saved from the demolition of the cathedral are the more than life-size crucifixes of 1520, which once filled the arch above the cathedral's rood screen right to the top of the vaulting.

Die überlebensgroßen Figuren der Triumphkreuzgruppe von 1520 aus dem leider abgebrochenen Goslarer Dom.

Weitere Kostbarkeiten sind der bronzene Krodoaltar aus dem 11. Jahrhundert, Glasmalereien und Gobelins aus dem Chorgestühl von 1519, Einzelfiguren und Flügelaltäre.

Einen Hinweis verdienen noch die mittelalterliche Küche und die Apotheke. Regelmäßig finden auch Sonderausstellungen zur Stadt-, Kunst- und Kulturgeschichte im Hause statt.

The more than life size crucifixes of 1520 once had their place in Goslar's cathedral, which unfortunately was demolished.

Other treasures on display are the bronze Krodoaltar of the 11th century, stained glass windows and Gobelins from the choir of 1519, and some statues and winged altar-pieces.

Last not least there are the medieval kitchen and pharmacy to look at. Special exhibitions that focus on the history of the city, the arts, and civilisation are held at regular intervals.

Das Zinnfigurenmuseum

19 Museen und Sammlungen gibt es in Goslar zu besichtigen. Sie umspannen vielfältige Themen von der Heimatkunde bis hin zu originellen Einzelobjekten wie z.B. Musikinstrumente und Puppen, Militaria der Goslarer Jäger, die Rüstkammer im Zwinger mit mittelalterlichen Waffen und Folterinstrumenten, das Museum für moderne Kunst im Mönchehaus, das Edelsteinmuseum im Ortsteil Hahnenklee und Erinnerungsstätten. Eines der Museen ist das Zinnfigurenmuseum in der Münzstraße.

Das Museum ist in einem Flügel des "Weißen Schwans" untergebracht, einem alten Ausspann, in dem früher Besucher mit Pferd und Wagen Unterschlupf fanden. Die Gastronomie in den übrigen Gebäuden, die sich um den romantischen Hof gruppieren, hält diese Tradition aufrecht. Die in fünf Jahrhunderten zusammengewachsenen Bauten sind dabei selbst ein recht anschauliches Fachwerkmuseum.

Die Zinnfigurenausstellung stellt in Dioramen Szenen aus der Goslarer Geschichte nach. Dabei wird anschaulich wie auf einer Theaterbühne das Geschehen deutlich gemacht, zum Beispiel die Entwicklung des Bergbaues im Rammelsberg, die Teufelsschlacht im Goslarer Dom, oder den Angriff Herzog Heinrichs von Braunschweig - ein Streit, der mit dem die Wirtschaftskraft der Stadt vernichtenden Diktatfrieden von 1552 endete. Aber auch Alltagsszenen im bürgerlichen Leben auf dem Markt, den Straßen, in Haus und Hof werden geschildert. Sonderausstellungen von Sammlern und Vereinen ergänzen das Museumsprogramm. In Fachkreisen gilt das Goslarer kulturhistorische Zinnfigurenmuseum als eines der bedeutendsten seiner Art.

The Pewter Figure Museum

There are 19 museums and collections to see in Goslar, covering a broad scope of topics from local heritage to rather singular specialities such as musical instruments or dolls, the history and equipment of the Goslar infantry or the armoury at the Zwinger with medieval weapons and torturing tools, the museum of modern arts at the Mönchehaus or the museum of gems and precious stones at Goslar Hahnenklee, and many more. One of these museums is the pewter museum in the Münzstraße.

The museum has found its place in a wing of the "Weißer Schwan" (White Swan), an old inn that once accommodated visitors with their horses and carts. Surrounding a very romantic courtyard, the restaurant and the hotel in the remaining old buildings still keep up that long tradition. Sharing a common history of over 500 years these buildings have come to be a rather fascinating museum of half-timbered architecture themselves.

With its many carefully designed and arranged dioramas, the Pewter Figure Museum endeavours to bring Goslar's history to life. Just like on a stage, events are being illustrated in great detail. One example is the history of mining in the Rammelsberg, another is the "Teufelsschlacht" (Fight with the devil) in Goslar's cathedral, or the attack of Duke Heinrich of Braunschweig (Brunswick) - the ensuing peace dictate of 1552 lost Goslar the mines and its economic backbone. But the dioramas also include scenes from everyday life, be it on the market or at home. Special exhibits by collectors and societies extend the museum's activities. Among experts, the Goslar Pewter Figure Museum with its focus on cultural history is considered one of the best of its kind.

| *Das Zinnfigurenmuseum im alten Ausspann in der Münzstraße.* | *The Pewter Figure Museum in the old inn in the Münzstraße.* |

| *Links: Angriff Herzog Heinrichs von Braunschweig auf die Stadt 1527.* | *Left: Duke Heinrich of Braunschweig (Brunswick) attacks the city in 1527.* |
| *Rechts: Die Grubenanlagen im Rammelsberg am Maltermeisterturm.* | *Right: The mines of the Rammelsberg at the Maltermeisterturm.* |

Häuserzeile am Liebfrauenberg

A row of houses at the Liebfrauenberg

Fachwerkhäuser

Wer auf seiner Wanderung durch die Straßen und Gassen Goslars vor den Patrizierhäusern innehält, nicht nur um sie zu betrachten, sondern auch, um mit den steinernen und hölzernen Zeugen vergangener Jahrhunderte historische Zwiesprache zu halten, wird sich immer wieder auch die Frage stellen, wie denn dies alles wurde, wie es wuchs, wie es blieb bis in unsere Gegenwart, und ob es wohl auch

Half-Timbered Houses

Any visitor who walks with open eyes and mind through the streets and alleys of Goslar will not only look at the splendour of the patrician houses. Listening to these witnesses of wood and stone and the stories they have to tell of centuries gone, he will sooner or later begin to wonder how all this once came about, how it grew, and how it survived until our days, and whether it will have a chance to go on

Die Peterstraße mit Wohnhäusern aus dem 15. bis 19. Jahrhundert.

The Peterstraße with its houses dating back to the 15th to 19th century.

Bestand haben wird in der Zukunft. Die Tradition im Wechselbad der Geschichte und der dauernde Strukturwandel einer Stadtgesellschaft gaben Goslar Ruhm und Glanz, Niedergang und Wiederaufstieg, geben dem Fragenden aber auch die Erkenntnis, nicht in einem verstaubten Geschichtsbuch zu blättern, das man mit dem hinteren Buchdeckel wieder zuschlägt, sondern die Gewißheit, daß

in the years to come. The ups and downs of a varying history, the constant changes in the make-up of a town culture and society contributed as much to Goslar's glory and splendour as they contributed to its downfall. So far Goslar has always managed to rise again. To walk the streets of Goslar means being face to face with living history. The houses along the streets are not the dusty covers of

Von 1530 bis 1620 herrscht im Fachwerkbau das Schmuckmotiv der "Sonnenrosenornamente" vor.	*Between 1530 and 1620 the sun ornaments were the dominating motif in ornamental carvings.*

dies alles noch lebt und daß in allen diesen Gebäuden Bürger unserer Zeit wohnen.

Die regelmäßige Holzkonstruktion des Fachwerks erschwert es, die Altersunterschiede leicht zu erkennen. Bei den noch aus dem Mittelalter stammenden Häusern kragen die Geschosse und die Traufe weit in den Straßenraum vor. Nur bescheidene Verzierungen finden sich auf den Geschoßschwellen. Ab 1550 wurden die Brüstungen in den Geschossen ganz mit Holz ausgefüllt. Dadurch standen große Flächen für die eingeschnitzten ornamentalen Schmuckformen zur Verfügung.

Zunächst waren dies vor allem "Sonnenrosenornamente" - Fächer- oder Muschelformen, sowie vielerlei symbolhafte Zeichen. Ab 1600 folgten "Metallornamente" - dem antiken Beschlagwerk entlehnte Muster - und schließlich Blumenranken als letztes

a mouldy history book but peopled by men living today and looking forward to tomorrow.

The regular structure in the woodwork of the half-timbered houses makes it difficult for the layman to distinguish their age. Buildings dating back to the Middle Ages usually are quite recognisable by their protruding upper storeys that overhang the street. Ornaments on the beams are mostly simple and rather few. But from 1550 onwards, the sills and panels of each storey were done completely in wood. This new design provided rather large areas for ornamental carvings.

In the beginning, the major ornaments were suns or palmettos and a large collection of symbols and similar signs. By about 1600 "metal ornaments", i.e. patterns taken from ancient examples, came into use. The last patterns to be used were of floral

Die Jakobistraße mit Häusern aus dem 15. bis 17. Jahrhundert.

The Jakobistraße with houses from the 15th to 17th century.

Häuser in der Bäckerstraße aus dem 16./17. Jahrhundert.

Houses in the Bäckerstraße date back to the 16th and 17th century.

Schnitzwerk. Danach sind es seit der Barockzeit nur noch mehr oder weniger umfangreiche Profilfolgen.

Das Fachwerk, dessen Schwarz-Weiß-Muster wir heute so schätzen, war einst der billigere Ersatz für einen Steinbau, den man sich nicht leisten konnte. Das wird besonders dort deutlich, wo man durch die Schmuckformen und Profile im Holz Steinquader vorgetäuscht hat. Ein gutes Beispiel dafür ist das Haus Bäckerstraße 3.

Heute haben sich die Kosten für einen Hausbau und das architektonische Verständnis der Bevölkerung umgekehrt. Stolz auf ihre Fachwerkhäuser, werden sie von ihren Eigentümern liebevoll gepflegt.

Der Schuhhof mit dem schlichten Gildehaus der Schuhmacher gehört zu

floral design. With the coming of the Baroque the highly ornamental design gave way to quite simple profiling.

The half-timbering whose black and white patterns we cherish so much today for its aesthetic qualities once was no more than the cheap substitute for a building in stone. This explains the conscious attempts to create the illusion of stone by carved profiles and ornaments. The house at Bäckerstraße 3 is an example for this.

Today the costs of building as well as the architectural understanding of the people are just the opposite. And so the owners of half-timbered houses are proud of their gems and care for them lovingly.

The Schuhhof with the plain guildhall of the shoemakers once was part of

Der Schuhhof, ein Rest des mittelalterlichen Marktes.

The Schuhhof is all that has remained of the medieval market square.

dem weitgehend bebauten alten Markt. Aus den mittelalterlichen Verkaufsständen der Händler und Handwerker, an die noch die Straßennamen Hoken-, Bäcker-, Fischemäkerstraße sowie Fleischscharren erinnern, sind schmale Buden geworden. Ihre Hausbreite wird bestimmt von dem ehemaligen Verkaufstisch, der zuerst mit einem Dach versehen, danach mehrfach aufgestockt worden ist. Die Häuserzeile zwischen dem Schuhhof und der Münzstraße ist ein gutes Beispiel für diese Hausentwicklung.

Dem Lauf der Gose verdankt Goslar den Namen, und mehrere Gosestraßen erinnern noch an den Bach. Dort, wo heute Wasser durch die Stadt fließt, heißt es nun Abzucht. Auf diese Merkwürdigkeit weiß mancher Ein-

the old market square, an area mostly built over today. It lives on in the names of streets and alleys such as Hoken-, Bäcker-, Fischemäkerstraße, or Fleischscharren [hawker, baker, fishmonger, butcher]. The houses in these streets also mirror this past. For when the stalls of the dealers and the craftsmen in course of time were given a roof, then a first storey, and then another storey, the size of the original counter decided the width of the later house. The rows of houses between Schuhhof and Münzstraße illustrate this development well.

While the town owes its name to the Gose creek whose name is kept alive in a number of "Gose"-streets, the open running waters in town are known by the name Abzucht. Even a lot of locals are hard put to explain

Partie an der Abzucht mit einem Mühlengerenne links.

Part of the Abzucht with a mill-run on the left.

heimische auch keine Antwort. Doch als der Bergbau oberhalb der Stadt sein Abwasser in die Gose einleitete, wurde diese als Trinkwasser unbrauchbar. Man baute deshalb einen Kanal, der die Gose oberhalb der Verschmutzung ableitete und so der Bevölkerung gutes Trinkwasser lieferte. Im dem alten Bachbett floß fortan das Abwasser aus den Gruben und auch aus der Stadt. So wurde der bergmännische Ausdruck "Abzucht" na-

this strange occurrence. Yet the explanation is quite simple. When the mines above the town started to leak their waste water into the Goose its water became unfit to drink. So a canal was built that diverted the creek uphill from the waste entry. Thus good drinking water could be supplied to the people. From then on, only the mine's waste waters ran in the old bed of the creek, soon to be joined by the town's sewage. So the miners' term

Das "rückschlächtige" Wasserrad der Lohmühle am Gemeindehof.

The overshot water-wheel of the Lohmühle at the Gemeindehof.

mensgebend für den Wasserlauf. Der meist unterirdisch verlaufende Gosekanal verschwand aus der Erinnerung.

27 Mühlen gab es einst an der Gose und an der Abzucht. Die Wasserkraft versorgte so vielerlei Betriebe mit Antriebsenergie. Heute ist nur noch ein sich drehendes Wasserrad in der Altstadt zu sehen. Es gehört zu einer Lohmühle, in der früher aus Rinden Gerbmittel hergestellt wurden.

for drainage, 'Abzucht', became the name for the open water. The underground Gose canal was forgotten.

Water-power was the main source of energy for many different businesses. In its heydays there once were 27 mills along the Gose and the Abzucht. Today only one turning water-wheel can still be seen in the old town. It belongs to a tanning mill that used to make tans from bark.

Die Stadtbefestigung

Zu einer Stadt gehörten Türme, Tore, Mauern und Wälle, deren Anlagen zusammen mit den Türmen der Kirchen das Gesicht einer Stadt prägten. Die Glocken der Kirchen riefen die frommen Bürger aber nicht nur zum Gebet und Gottesdienst zusammen, sondern läuteten Sturm, wenn feindliche Heerhaufen sich der Stadt näherten oder Feuersbrünste durch die Straßen fegten. Wenn am Abend die Stadttore geschlossen wurden, fühlte sich der Bürger in seiner Stadtburg geborgen und sicher.

So hatten diese burgenartigen Türme, Tore und Mauern eine doppelte Bedeutung für die Stadt. Sie sollten nicht nur Schutz bieten gegen feindliche Überfälle, Angriffe und Belagerungen, sondern waren zugleich sichtbares Zeichen der Selbständigkeit und des Selbstbewußtseins des Bürgers der Stadt und damit der Bürgerschaft.

Als allerdings die Befestigungswerke im 16. Jahrhundert schließlich vollendet waren, da brauchte man sie nicht mehr. Die Feuerwaffe war erfunden. Schwere Geschütze wurden jetzt aufgefahren, die, von einem Büchsenmeister geleitet, mächtige Eisenkugeln mit Pulverkraft hinauszuschleudern vermochten, so daß selbst dickste Mauern keinen Schutz mehr bieten konnten.

Von den einst vier großen Stadttoren ist das im Osten gelegene Breite Tor am besten erhalten. Die Kaiserfiguren, die die Ankommenden begrüßen, vertraten hier den Herrn der kaiserlich-freien Reichsstadt und dienten zugleich zur Abschreckung von Angreifern.

Seite 63: Das Breite Tor im Osten der Altstadt.

The Town Fortifications

Any medieval town had to have its towers, gates, walls and moats. Together with the towers of the churches they created the unmistakable face of a town. The bells of the churches not only called the citizens to the church, they also rang an alarm when hostile forces approached the town or when fires stormed through the streets and threatened to destroy the city. When the town gates were closed at night, the burghers withdrew into their houses feeling safe and secure inside their fortress.

Thus those castle like towers, gates, and walls had a double meaning for the town. On the one hand they were to provide protection against any sort of hostile assault and siege. On the other hand they served as a visible symbol of the independence and self-confidence of the individual citizen and the town as a whole.

But when the fortifications of the city had eventually been completed during the 16th century, they had already been rendered obsolete by the invention of gunpowder. From then on more and more potent canons were brought before a town, and if guided well by an experienced officer, their fire was so effective that even the thickest walls could offer only little protection.

Of Goslar's four major gates, the one to the east, the Breite Tor (Broad Gate), has survived with the least damage. The statues of the emperors that great the traveller on the one hand represented the rulers of the imperial city, on the other hand they were to deter any would-be attackers.

Page 63: The Breite Tor (Broad Gate) at the eastern end of the old town.

Links: Kaiser als Oberherren der Stadt begrüßen an allen Toren die Gäste.

Rechts: Der Brunnen am Breiten Tor markiert das Ende einer hölzernen Wasserleitung.

Left: Stressing direct imperial rule, statues of the emperors greet the visitors to the city at every gate.

Right: The fountain at the Breites Tor (Broad Gate) marks the end of a wooden water pipe.

Wo das Wasser die Stadt durch die Befestigungsmauer verließ, ergaben sich Schwachstellen im Verteidigungssystem. Ein solches "Wasserloch" in der Nähe des St. Annenwalles ist dafür ein anschauliches Beispiel.

Wie für eine Burganlage schützen Mauern und Türme den Durchlaß, der außerdem noch durch Fallgatter versperrt war. An dieser bemerkenswerten Stelle treffen fünf Wasserläufe zusammen: Die Abzucht, ein Mühlgraben, das Wallwasser, die Wasserbreeke und der tiefste Entwässerungsstollen aus dem Rammelsberg.

Aus den Wallanlagen ist ein Grüngür-

Wherever water entered or left the town by way of the town walls, the defensive position was weakened. The "waterhole" near the St. Annenwall is a good example for the problems arising from this situation.

Similar to the defences of a castle, walls and towers fortify the water's passage way which also could be blocked by portcullis. Five waters meet at this remarkable place: the Abzucht, a mill-run, the creek Wasserbreeke, and the deepest of the drainage tunnels from the Rammelsberg mines.

The walls have since been turned into

Das Wasserloch, der Ausfluß der Ab-
zucht aus der Stadt.

The Wasserloch (Waterhole) where
the Abzucht leaves the old town.

Die Stadtmauer mit den Wallanlagen am Kegelworthturm (links) und an der Glockengießerstraße (rechts).

The town wall and its fortifications at the Kegelworthturm (left) and the Glockengießerstraße (right).

tel geworden, der zum Teil aus öffentlichen Anlagen, überwiegend jedoch aus Privatgärten besteht, in denen es in der warmen Jahreszeit grünt und blüht.

Im Kranz der mittelalterlichen Befestigungsanlagen steht der mit 6,5 m Mauerstärke mächtigste Zwingerturm. Er beherbergt heute ein Restaurant, romantische Ferienwohnungen und die "Rüstkammer" mit der Ausstellung von historischen Waffen und Folterwerkzeugen. Von seinem Dach aus hat man einen weiten Blick über die Altstadt und das Umland. Von dem einstigen Wassergraben ist hier mit dem Kahnteich ein Stück erhalten geblieben.

Zu den ältesten Bauten gehören die Schalentürme, die halbrund vor die Stadtmauer heraustreten. Zur Stadtseite waren sie nur durch eine Fachwerkwand geschlossen, weil man von

a green belt. While some of it is public parkland, most of it are private gardens. Well tended by their owners they are a colourful sight during the warmer part of the year.

With walls about 6,5 metres (21½ feet) thick, the Zwinger is the strongest and most impressive of the medieval towers. Still reminiscent of its former past is the "armoury", a museum of historic weapons and torturing tools. Less martial uses today are a restaurant and some most romantic holiday apartments. Great sights over the old town and the surrounding country are afforded from the roof of the tower. The Kahnteich is a remnant of the former moat.

The flanking towers are among the oldest parts of the town's fortifications. Protruding from the wall in a half circle, their townward side was closed of by a simple half-timbered wall because

66

Der Zwinger am Thomaswall, 1514 er-baut, einst mächtigster Geschützturm. | *The Zwinger at the Thomaswall, built in 1514, once the strongest gun tower.*

Der Weberturm an der Mauerstraße (links) und der Wachtmeisterturm am Vititor (rechts).

The Weberturm at the Mauerstraße (left) and the Wachtmeisterturm at the Vititor (right).

dort aus keinen Angriff erwartete. Erhalten und verteidigt wurden die Türme einst von Handwerkerverbänden, die ihnen den Namen gegeben haben, hier z.B. der Weberturm. Heute werden einige davon als originelle Wohnungen genutzt: in jedem Geschoß ein Raum!

Die vier wichtigsten Tore der Stadtmauer von Goslar waren das Rosentor, das Klaustor, das Vititor und das Breite Tor. Der Flankierungszwinger des Rosentores wurde 1508 für die damals neu aufkommenden Feuerwaffen mit rund 5 m dicken Mauern erbaut. In ihm ist heute das Hotel "Der Achtermann" untergebracht. Aus den Batteriedecks des Mittelalters wurden Räume mit behaglichen Nischen, deren Schießschartenfenster noch an deren alte Aufgabe erinnern. 1982 wurde der Komplex um ein modernes Tagungszentrum erweitert.

nobody expected an attack from that direction. The upkeep and defense of these towers once was the duty of the guilds who gave them their names, hence for example the Weberturm (Weavers' Tower). Today some of them are used as unique living quarters: one room per storey!

The four most important gates in the walls of Goslar were the Rosentor, the Klaustor, the Vititor, and the Breites Tor. The flanking tower of the Rosentor, built in 1508, was given 5 m thick walls to withstand the cannons then being introduced to warfare. Today it is part of the hotel "Der Achtermann". The medieval battery floors have been turned into cosy rooms whose loophole windows still remind the guest of the earlier purpose of his resting place. In 1982 a modern convention centre was added to the old buildings.

Der Achtermann, ein Flankierungs-
zwinger des ehemaligen Rosentores.

The Achtermann, a flanking tower of
the former Rosentor.

Das Breite Tor hinterläßt bis heute einen großartigen Eindruck von seiner Wehrhaftigkeit. Es bestand aus einer Hofanlage, dessen äußeres Tor im Verlauf der Feldmauer und dessen bis heute erhaltenes inneres Tor in der Stadtmauer stand. Zwischen beiden steht die mittelalterliche Söldnerkaserne.

Über der Durchfahrt befand sich eine Kapelle, die den Reisenden vor und

Up to this very day, the Breite Tor (Broad Gate) leaves a grand impression of its earlier defensive capabilities. The gate was comprised of a courtyard whose outer gate was part of a bailey and whose inner gate was part of the town wall. Between them there stood the barracks for the medieval garrison.

Above the gate there was a chapel for the travellers to pray for guidance at

Links: Überreste vom Rosentor.

Rechts: Der Teufelsturm an der Mauerstraße.

Left: Remains of the Rosentor.

Right: The Teufelsturm (Devil's Tower) at the Mauerstraße.

nach der Fahrt zum Bitt- und Dankgebet einlud. Kaiserfiguren schmückten die gewaltigen Außenwände der mächtigen Bollwerke, die als Sinnbilder der kaiserlich-freien Stellung anzusehen sind.

Die Stadtbürger haben ihre Befestigungsanlagen niemals als eine Last empfunden, sondern als notwendigen Schutz ihres Stadtwesens und als imponierende Darstellung der Stadtfreiheit.

Die Gilden und Zünfte haben einst die Türme erbaut, sie sorgten für deren Erhaltung und stellten die Besatzung. Deshalb tragen viele auch den Namen dieser Handwerker: Weber, Knochenhauer, Schmiede, usw.

Durch die Tore flutete am Tage ein reges Leben. Reisende Kaufleute, Fuhrleute mit ihren Handelswagen, Reiter, walzende Gesellen und fah-

their departure and to say thanks after their return. The statues of the emperors adorning the massive outer walls of these bulwarks are symbols of the town's independence and direct imperial rule.

The townsfolk never saw the upkeep of their fortifications as a burden, but rather as an unavoidable necessity to guarantee the safety of their town. Yet it was also an expression of their pride in the freedom a town offered.

The guilds once build the towers of the walls, took care of their upkeep and manned them in times of need. Therefore most of the towers are named after their trades: weavers, butchers, smiths, and so on.

In the daytime a lot of traffic flowed back and forth through the gates. Travelling salesmen, carters with their wagons full of goods, riders, journey-

Der "Werderhof", die mittelalterliche Söldnerkaserne am Breiten Tor.

The "Werderhof", the medieval barracks at the Breite Tor.

rende Schüler zogen ein und aus, und bevor am Abend die aus mächtigen Balken hergestellten Fallgitter heruntergelassen wurden, schlüpften noch die Bürger hindurch, die vor der Mauer ihr bescheidenes Stück Ackerland besorgt hatten. Ruhe und Frieden kehrten in die Stadt ein. Man konnte nur noch das gleichmäßige Stapfen der Stadtsoldaten hören, die auf Nachtwache gezogen waren.

men, and travelling scholars. And before the heavy portcullis were lowered for the night, the last to pass through were some of the townsfolk returning from their small plot of land outside the townwalls. Then peace and quiet slowly began to settle over the town. Only the steady marching steps of the town's soldiers on their night guard duty disturbed the silence now and then.

Die Übertageanlagen des Rammels-
berger Bergbaues.

The surface installations of the Ram-
melsberg mine.

Der Rammelsberg

Goslars Schicksal war immer eng mit dem Erzbergbau im Rammelsberg verbunden, über 3000 Jahre wurde hier Bergbau betrieben. Der Erzreichtum ließ im 10. und 11. Jahrhundert die einst größte Stadt in Norddeutschland entstehen. Kaiser und Könige residierten zu Füßen des Berges. Im Streit um den Besitz der Gruben zwischen Bürgertum und Fürstenherrschaft unterlag Goslar.

Der Bergbau hatte selbst ein mehrfaches Wechselspiel zwischen reicher und armer Ausbeute. Der Abbau erreichte mehrmals die Grenzen seiner technischen Möglichkeiten. Dazu gehörten vor allem die Bewältigung der sich sammelnden Wassermengen in den Tiefen und die Fördermechaniken. Fast 100 Jahre, von 1486 bis 1585, baute man zum Beispiel an dem tiefsten Julius-Fortunatus-Stollen, um die Wassernot zu beseitigen.

Nach der Erschöpfung der Erzvorräte nach mehr als 3000 Jahren Abbau gehört der Rammelsberg heute zum Weltkulturerbe. Bei einer Besichtigung des Museums kann man die Entwicklung der Technik seit dem Mittelalter und die Arbeitswelt der Bergleute anschaulich erleben.

Die Bedeutung dieser Anlage für Besucher und Wissenschaftler liegt darin, daß der Übergang vom Erzabbau in den Gruben zum Bergbaumuseum nahtlos erfolgen konnte und hier Spuren der Arbeit aus dem Zeitraum von 3000 Jahren sichtbar erhalten geblieben sind.

In dem nach seinem Schöpfer benannten Röderstollen sind die alten Wasserkraftanlagen mit den gewaltigen Rädern und den Gestängen, Seilzügen und Wasserläufen zu besichtigen. Das Feuergezähergewölbe aus dem 12./13. Jahrhundert ist vermutlich

The Rammelsberg

Throughout its history, the fate of Goslar has always been closely connected to the mines of the Rammelsberg. For more than 3000 years mining took place.In the 10th and 11th century, the rich ore bodies once made northern Germany largest and most prosperous town where emperors and kings liked to reside. Later the feuds with the nobles over the control of the mines lead to the downfall of the city.

The mines themselves lived through numerous ups and downs of rich finds and meagre gains. Time and again the limits were set by the geological and technological conditions. Delving deeper and deeper, one of the main difficulties was the draining of the mines that were continuously threatened by flooding. It took almost one hundred years, from 1486 to 1585, to dig the deepest Julius-Fortunatus-Stollen to cope with the waters.

After more than 3000 years of continuous mining the veins were finally exhausted. But still the Rammelsberg mine lives on. Now a museum, it provides an intensive hands-on experience of the development of mining and a miner's working life from the Middle Ages up to our times.

The great benefit for visitors and scientists alike is the fact that quite different from other cases, the changeover from active mine to museum took place without much interruption. So the traces of work from over three thousand years were not lost and could be preserved more easily.

Named after its builder, the Röder Gallery served as a water supply tunnel for the huge underground waterwheels. The water-runs as well as the wheels, rods and ropes can still be seen. The Feuergezähergewölbe, an immense vault dug in the 12th and

Links: Die Grubenbahn führt heute Besucher in den Berg zu alten Abbaustätten.

Rechts: Gestänge und Seilzüge dienten der Kraftübertragung zwischen den Wasserrädern und den Förderanlagen.

Left: Visitors ride the mine train into the mountain to see the old medieval mining sites.

Right: The rods and pulleys were once used to transmit the power generated by the waterwheels to the hoists at the shafts.

der älteste erhaltene Grubenraum in Europa. Im Bereich des Ratstiefstenstollens aus der gleichen Zeit faszinieren die farbenprächtigen Vitriole, Oxidationsprodukte der verschiedenen Erzarten.

Mit der Grubenbahn gelangt man in den neuzeitlichen Abbaubereich. Hier wird die Entwicklung der Abbautechnik von der schweren Handarbeit mit Schlägel und Eisen bis zum maschinellen Betrieb mit Bohrern, Sprengungen und dem Verladen des gewonnenen Erzes vorgeführt.In den letzten Jahren ist im Rammelsberg eine Fülle neuer Exponate und Angebote geschaffen worden – von verschiedenen Führungstouren bis zum Museumsrestaurant. Ein Besuch lohnt sich immer!

13th century, is probably the oldest surviving chamber of a mine in Europe. The Ratstiefstenstollen, dug in the same period, offers a fascinating variety colourful vitriols, the sulphates of different ores.

An underground mine train takes the visitors to the newer sections. Here the important stages in the development of mining technology are presented from the hard manual labour just with iron and hammer on to the mechanical drilling and the use of explosives. In the last years, a variety of new items and offers was developed in the Rammelsberg – from different guided tours to a museum restaurant. A visit is always worth it!

Eines der großen Wasserräder im Röderstollen unter Tage.

One of the large underground water-wheels at the Röder Gallery.

Öffnungszeiten der Goslarer Museen und Sehenswürdigkeiten
Opening Hours of Goslar´s Museums und Attractions

Weltkulturerbe Rammelsberg		täglich / daily	09.00 - 18.00
Museum/Besucherbergwerk	Tel. (0 53 21) 75 01 22	außer 24. und 31. Dezember	
Bergtal 19	Fax (0 53 21) 75 01 30		
(Seite/Page 72-75)			
Kaiserpfalz	April - Oktober:	täglich / daily	10.00 - 17.00
Kaiserbleek 6	November - März:	täglich / daily	10.00 - 16.00
(Seite/Page 14-19)	Tel. (0 53 21) 3 11 96 93		
	Fax (0 53 21) 3 11 06 99		
Huldigungssaal	Januar - Dezember	täglich / daily	11.00 - 16.00
Markt 1	Tel. (0 53 21) 70 42 41		
(Seite/Page 22/23)	Fax (0 53 21) 75 78 75		
Goslarer Museum	April - Oktober	Di. - So.	10.00 - 17.00
Königstraße 1	November - März	Di. - So.	10.00 - 16.00
(Seite/Page 50/51)	Tel. (0 53 21) 4 33 94		
	Fax (0 53 21) 75 78 75		
Großes Heiliges Kreuz	Januar - Dezember	täglich / daily	11.00 - 17.00
Hoher Weg 7	Tel. (0 53 21) 2 18 00		
(Seite/Page 42)			
St. Annenhaus	November - März	Mo. - Do.	11.00 - 13.00
Glockengießerstraße 65	November - März	Mo. - Do.	14.00 - 16.00
(Seite/Page 43/44)	April - Oktober	Mo. - Do.	14.00 - 17.00
	Januar - Dezember	Fr. - Sa.	11.00 - 13.00
	Tel. (0 53 21) 39 87 00 und		
	(0 53 21) 2 47 62		
Siemenshaus	Januar - Dezember	Di. u. Do.	9.00 - 12.00
Schreiberstraße 12	Gruppenführungen auf Anfrage		
(Seite/Page 46/47)	Tel. (0 53 21) 2 38 37		
Mönchehaus	Januar - Dezember	Di. - Sa.	10.00 - 17.00
Mönchestraße 3	Januar - Dezember	So.	10.00 - 13.00
(Seite/Page 48/49)	Tel. (0 53 21) 2 95 70 und		
	(0 53 21) 49 48		
Zinnfigurenmuseum	Januar - Dezember	täglich / daily	10.00 - 17.00
Münzstraße 11	Tel. (0 53 21) 2 58 89		
(Seite/Page 52/53)			
Museum im Zwinger	März	täglich / daily	10.00 - 16.00
Thomasstraße 2	April - Mitte November	täglich / daily	10.00 - 17.00
(Seite/Page 67)	Mitte November - Februar	geschlossen	
	Tel. (0 53 21) 4 31 40		
Musikinstrumente- und	Januar - Dezember	täglich / daily	11.00 - 17.00
Puppenmuseum	Tel. (0 53 21) 2 69 45		
Hoher Weg 5			

Stand der Angaben Juli 2003, Änderungen vorbehalten.
Information correct as of Juli 2003 but subject to change without notice.

Sonnenuntergang am Breiten Tor. | *Sunset at the Breite Tor.*

VERLAG SCHADACH
LITERATUR AUS DEM HARZ

Gutenbergstraße 3, 38640 Goslar, Tel. (0 53 21) 2 56 77, Fax 4 03 58
Internet: www.verlag-schadach.de   E-Mail: info@verlag-schadach.de